SOMETHING BLUE

by Gill Adams

JOSEF WEINBERGER PLAYS

LONDON

SOMETHING BLUE
First published in 2002
by Josef Weinberger Ltd
12-14 Mortimer Street, London, W1T 3JJ

ISBN 0 85676 261 X

This play is protected by Copyright. According to Copyright Law, no public performance or reading of a protected play or part of that play may be given without prior authorisation from Josef Weinberger Plays, as agent for the Copyright Owners.

From time to time it is necessary to restrict or even withdraw the rights of certain plays. **It is therefore essential to check with us before making a commitment to produce a play.**

NO PERFORMANCE MAY BE GIVEN WITHOUT A LICENCE

AMATEUR PRODUCTIONS
Royalties are due at least thirty days prior to the first performance. A royalty quotation will be issued upon receipt of the following details:

Name of Licensee
Play Title
Place of Performance
Dates and Number of Performances
Audience Capacity
Ticket Prices

PROFESSIONAL PRODUCTIONS
All enquiries regarding stock and repertory rights in the English Language (excluding the United States and Canada), German Language and Scandinavian territories should be addressed to Josef Weinberger Plays at the address above. Enquiries concerning all other rights should be addressed to the Curtis Brown Group Ltd, 4th Floor, Haymarket House, 28/29 Haymarket, London, SW1Y 4SP.

OVERSEAS PRODUCTIONS
Applications for productions overseas should be addressed to our local authorised agents. Further details are listed in our catalogue of plays, published every two years, or available from Josef Weinberger Plays at the address above.

Printed by Watkiss Studios Ltd, Biggleswade, Beds, England

“Love hath a language of his own – A voice that goes from heart to heart – whose mystic tone Love only knows”

The Silent Voice by Thomas Moore, 1837

SOMETHING BLUE was first performed at the Stephen Joseph Theatre, Scarborough, on 5th March 2002, with the following cast:

JOHNNY	Bryan Kennedy
MANDY	Tracy Sweetinburgh
PAM	Amanda Abbington
SANDRA	Sally George
VERA	Gillian Wright

Directed by Laura Harvey
Designed by Pip Leckenby

For my brother Ricky and my best friend Mandy – 'cos God knows it's never easy following your heart.

With special big thanks to Laura Harvey, Alan Ayckbourn, Neil Rider, Will Kerley, Averil Coult, Barbara Laverack, my lovely daughter Lucy and my dad for putting up with me, and Kate Rowland, for that special 'Rowland Magic'.

ACT ONE

Scene One

As the audience settles, a horse-drawn carriage can be heard. A bell chimes three times. The voice of the Prime Minister, Tony Blair, can be heard.

TONY BLAIR How many times shall we remember her, in how many different ways? With the sick, the dying, with children, with the needy – when, with just a look or a gesture that spoke so much more than words, she would reveal to all of us the depth of her compassion and her humanity.

(*In the darkness, a match is struck and three candles are lit in front of an elaborate but stylish shrine to Princess Diana.*)

How difficult things were for her from time to time, surely we can only guess at – but the people everywhere, not only here in Britain, but everywhere, they kept faith with Princess Diana, they liked her, they loved her, they regarded her as one of the people.

(*Appropriate music plays.*)

Scene Two

Saturday, 6th September 1997. 9.00 AM. The setting is a trendy high street hairdressers in Beverley – a small northern market town near Hull.

JOHNNY *finishes lighting the candles and crosses himself in Catholic fashion.*

JOHNNY You'll never know how special you was . . . still are to me . . . I can't believe you've gone . . .

(MANDY, PAM'S *best friend and only bridesmaid, waddles in carrying carrier bags. She is heavily pregnant but already a big girl.*)

MANDY Eh up, Johnny boy . . . what the 'ell you doing?

JOHNNY Mandy . . . ? You're early . . . I'm, er . . . just, you know, paying my respects . . .

MANDY How you gonna do our hair in the dark?

(JOHNNY *is slightly put out that* MANDY *has arrived before he has had chance to say a few words in private. He takes her carrier bags.*)

JOHNNY I'm not barmy . . . 'ere, let me take your bags . . . Blimey, what the hell you got here?

MANDY Half my Dave's Mam's fridge . . . well, I'm eating for three now!

(*He heads off to take them out to the kitchen – The lights come on.*)

JOHNNY (*shouts, off*) I thought you always did. (*Laughs.*) I'll put 'em in the fridge – you want a coffee?

MANDY I'd love one, Johnny – but the smell of coffee makes me gag.

JOHNNY How about tea?

MANDY I can't stand tea either, there's some Lucozade in the other bag. Dave's Mam keeps buying me it, I've told her I'm not poorly, I'm just pregnant but she won't listen. Mother-in-Laws, I swear to God, Pam doesn't know what she's letting herself in for . . .

(MANDY *looks at the picture of Diana.*)

MANDY Wink if you agree . . .

(*She lights a fag with one of the candles.* JOHNNY *comes back – horrified she's smoking.*)

JOHNNY You're smoking!

MANDY Nice frame. Real silver, is it?

JOHNNY Yes, solid silver from Saks, New York, so keep your hands off it! And you shouldn't even be smoking in your condition!

(*She ignores him.* JOHNNY *picks up the tin waste bin – with a look of distinct distaste he takes the cigarette off her and stubs it out.*)

MANDY Oh don't start preaching to me, Johnny! With my hormones all to cock I'm likely to deck you – am I early or are the others late?

JOHNNY (*put out*) You're early. Don't know why, I'm doing you last.

MANDY Last?

JOHNNY I've had strict orders to do Pam's first and Vera's second.

MANDY Can I go on the sun bed, then?

JOHNNY No, you can't . . .

MANDY What about a body wrap?

JOHNNY (*his face says it all*) You can't have anything, Mandy, there's only me in today.

MANDY Well that's a bit daft, isn't it?

JOHNNY Probably, but that's how it is today . . .

(MANDY *helps herself to a handful of marshmallows off the reception coffee table.*)

MANDY I might have a nap, actually. I'm not sleeping very well.

JOHNNY I know. Ever since I heard the news I've been in shock . . .

(MANDY *nearly chokes on a marshmallow – begins to cough, takes a glass of water off the reception desk and drinks it.* JOHNNY *doesn't say anything but stares at her in disbelief as she sips the water.*)

MANDY Oooh, don't start me on that one, Dave's mother's been driving us mad. She's locked herself in the back bedroom with the portable telly and Dave's fishing flask full of sweet tea.

JOHNNY I don't blame her . . .

MANDY I wouldn't mind, she doesn't even take sugar. She's got two ultra-soft bog rolls and a bumper box of Black Magic. She said she's not coming downstairs till Sunday night. Selfish cow. What are you looking at?

JOHNNY Nothing . . . Only that was Lourdes water, that's all.

MANDY You what?

JOHNNY (*exasperated*) I said it's holy water . . .

MANDY Good, 'cos I've got shocking heartburn.

JOHNNY (*snaps*) Oh, well, go on then, why don't you just swig it back!

(*She does.* PAM *walks in, carrying a hatbox with her veil in it.* PAM *is a trendy twenty year old. Both her and* MANDY *are care workers at the same old people's home, and she is still wearing her tunic.*)

PAM She driving you mad already? Hiya, Johnny!

(*He kisses her cheek and takes the hatbox.*)

JOHNNY Hiya, Pammy.

MANDY How you doin', kid?

JOHNNY Oh, is this the veil?

(JOHNNY *starts to lift the lid – she stops him.*)

PAM Oh, no, don't get it out . . . it's too early . . . I don't think me belly can take it right now . . .

JOHNNY (*put out*) Oh right, sorry . . . you're OK, though?

PAM Yeah, course I am, why shouldn't I be?

JOHNNY I'll shove kettle on . . . yeah?

PAM Thanks.

MANDY God, he's a bit OTT, in't he? You know, about Saint Diana . . .

PAM He liked her, Mandy, a lot of people did . . . and anyway I suppose it's bringing it all back for him . . .

MANDY Bringing what back?

PAM You know what, his Jimmy died and that . . .

MANDY Yeah . . . but that was ages ago, you'd think he'd have got over it by now.

PAM Well he obviously hasn't, so keep it shut, alright?

(*As* JOHNNY *comes back,* PAM *is looking at the shrine.*)

PAM So? Great day to get wed, isn't it?

JOHNNY I know. You gonna be alright, though? You haven't been to work, have you?

PAM Only for a couple of hours. I've been covering fatso's shift, haven't I? 'Ere, Scotch Jock had a funny turn on the lav again, Mand.

MANDY He puts it on, Pam, so you catch him with his drawers down.

PAM Rubbish.

MANDY She's a sucker for all his pervy tricks . . .

PAM He just misses Little Betty.

JOHNNY Aw, is Little Betty his 'wee wife'?

MANDY No, Little Betty was his 'wee' gambling partner. Deaf as dormouse and as blind as a kebab.

PAM (*laughs*) Ignore her . . .

MANDY It's true, fastest shuffler in Sunny Bank, she was.

JOHNNY Aw, bless.

MANDY Bless my arse! When she heard Scotch Jock opening the games cupboard, she'd be off on that Zimmer like greased lightening!

JOHNNY No!

MANDY I tell you, no one was safe.

PAM Well, I liked her . . .

MANDY You like everyone. Six hours later she'd be taking the old sod for every button he had. We had to hide the scissors. Didn't we, Pam?

PAM They were good friends, Mandy. He misses her, that's all. So do I.

JOHNNY You look a bit stressed, Pam.

(*They both look at Diana's photo.*)

PAM Oh, don't worry about me. I just hope me Mother gets here on time.

JOHNNY She's definitely coming, is she?

MANDY Aye, she is, so you'd better get the first aid box ready . . .

PAM Ignore her, she's just trying to wind me up.

MANDY No, Pam. I'm just reminding you of the error of your ways – she hasn't told the lovely Vera yet!

JOHNNY You haven't?

PAM How could I? She's been so . . .

MANDY Demented?

PAM Excited . . . I just didn't want to spoil things for her.

MANDY No? So why ask your mother to come, then?

JOHNNY Why do you think?

MANDY I have no idea.

JOHNNY When was you thinking of telling her?

PAM You've seen what Vera's been like, Johnny . . . I've never seen her so happy . . .

MANDY 'Course she's happy, Pam, she's getting her own way . . .

PAM Not totally . . .

(*They both look at* PAM.)

PAM I'm gonna tell her as soon as she gets here . . . get it over with . . .

(MANDY *and* JOHNNY *both look at one another knowingly.* PAM *walks over to the shrine.*)

PAM You know what I was thinking this morning? I mean the minute me eyes opened . . . you'd think it would 'ave been about the wedding, wouldn't yer? . . .

MANDY Yeah, well I tell you what I was thinking – I hope to God I still fit into me frock . . .

JOHNNY Mandy, give it a rest, eh?

PAM . . . I thought how horrible it must be for Diana's sons. They 'ad to go to bed last night knowing that they were gonna have to face all this today . . . I mean, how brave must they be, eh? Knowing they're never gonna see her again?

JOHNNY They have no choice, Pam . . .

PAM Brides are meant to feel special on their wedding day, aren't they? They're meant to wake up excited . . .

JOHNNY Do you feel a bit sad?

MANDY Or a bit insane, even? 'Cos I'm telling you that's actually quite normal . . .

PAM I don't feel anything . . . I'm not sad. I'm not happy. I'm not even sure I feel like me any more . . .

JOHNNY I think that's just nerves – 'cos of your Mam coming . . .

MANDY Aye, nerves and intense fear . . . very natural, is that . . .

(PAM *looks at Diana.*)

PAM It must 'ave been love, you know . . . I mean 'er marrying Big Ears, they say love is blind, don't they?

(JOHNNY *looks at* MANDY.)

JOHNNY Yeah, they certainly do . . .

PAM But if he'd been just an ordinary bloke that drove a bus or summat, I wonder if she'd 'ave married him? Or even fancied him . . . ?

MANDY I doubt it . . .

PAM (*laughs – painful*) You know when she found out he was in love with another woman, she didn't want to marry him. She wanted to cancel, but her sister said she couldn't 'cos the tea-towels 'ad been printed. (*Laughs.*) Bloody tea-towels, I ask yer . . . !

MANDY Aye, I know my Dave's mam's got one of them . . . two weeks ago it was hung on the washing line, now it's in a bloody frame! How weird is that?

(JOHNNY *exits to the beauty room.*)

JOHNNY It's not weird, Mandy, she was adored by millions.

MANDY I do know that . . . but if you ask me it's still bloody weird, in't it, Pam?

PAM Mandy, can't you please just try and be a nicer, warmer, more charming person today? Else I'll hide all your little snacks and ban you from the finger buffet . . .

MANDY I thought it was a six-course sit-down meal?

PAM It is . . . but in the other room it's a finger buffet.

MANDY I thought it was in a marquee?

PAM It is . . .

MANDY So what's this other room? For kids?

PAM Kids are banned.

MANDY And?

PAM There are fire regulations, you know . . .

MANDY Yeah, and so who's in the other room? Arsonists?

PAM The numbers were too high, that's all. It's better then leaving people out.

MANDY People? What people?

PAM It's for Mickey and my friends, distant relatives, you know how it is . . .

MANDY Do I?

PAM The marquee only seats a hundred.

MANDY And who the fuck are they?

PAM Mandy, I don't need this . . .

MANDY And how many does the other room hold?

(*Pause.*)

PAM Twenty-five.

MANDY So am I one of the hundred or one of the twenty-five? Pam?

PAM What do you think?

MANDY I don't know. Well, let me think. I am your maid of honor. I am your best friend, but I am fat and eating for three . . .

PAM You're on the big table with me.

MANDY So, basically, Vera and 'the chosen ones' are tucking into a six-course sit-down meal in the marquee and your friends are shoved away in some other room eating a finger buffet?

PAM You make it sound terrible. Mandy, a finger buffet in that place is –

MANDY Is what?

PAM Still impressive.

MANDY Oh, well, that's alright then. They'll consider themselves lucky then, won't they?

PAM Drop it . . .

MANDY It's only *your* wedding.

PAM Why you doing this?

MANDY . . . I mean, what say do you have in it?

PAM I said drop it, alright!

MANDY I suppose love is blind, eh?

PAM I'm not listening . . .

MANDY Even for Vera it's mean, and you know it!

(PAM *stands and walks over to the shrine – changes the subject. A beat.*)

PAM Nice frame, bit over the top though, don't you think?

MANDY (*snaps*) What do I think?

PAM Yeah.

MANDY You mean to say my opinion actually matters to you?

PAM Forget it . . .

MANDY I think the world's filled with people who are either liars or being lied to!

PAM What?

MANDY The car crash . . . I think it was no bloody accident!

PAM Shut up, stupid!

MANDY Stupid?

PAM Yes, you're talking rubbish.

MANDY So, I'm fat and stupid. Are you sure I'm marquee material? Are you sure Vera wouldn't prefer me in the other room?

(JOHNNY *walks back – overhearing.*)

JOHNNY It's not a day to fight, girls . . .

MANDY 'Ere Johnny, is Vera having one of them body wraps?

JOHNNY Vera's having the works . . .

MANDY Well when she's stripped and wrapped and ready to go in the microwave – I thought I'd take her photo.

PAM What?

JOHNNY She means the Swedish body wrap.

MANDY Posh name for a bit of mud and cling film.

PAM Bloody hell, Mandy, no! She'll go ballistic. Stay out of trouble and I'll fetch you a bacon butty. One. Without butter.

MANDY When?

PAM Later.

MANDY Make it now and I'll even smile all day.

PAM You should want to – it is my wedding.

MANDY Tell 'em to keep the rind on and make sure it's crispy, top cake dipped in tomato and bottom in them greasy mushrooms they do, ta – oh, and loads of mustard and brown sauce and loads of vinegar. I think I must be craving acid . . .

JOHNNY Oh! Please someone rush out for one, quick!

MANDY Well you heard him . . . can't you make it two?

(PAM *exits, laughing.*)

PAM No, you're already pushing your luck having one!

MANDY She's a total star, that one. Do you know I would rip apart with my bare hands anyone who hurt her.

JOHNNY Really? What a great chum you are!

MANDY Whilst she's out shall we put the telly on and have a good weep?

JOHNNY No . . . Shall I pluck them eyebrows of yours?

MANDY Will it hurt?

JOHNNY Definitely, but it's not as painful as us having to look at 'em in that state.

MANDY Shall we arm wrestle?

JOHNNY Shall I bounce on your belly like a trampoline?

MANDY Shall I smack you in your puffy chops?

JOHNNY You really are an appalling excuse for a woman.

MANDY Yeah, and you're just appalling . . .

(VERA *swans in holding several classy carrier bags including Harvey Nichols and, of course, Harrods. She's in her fifties – disguised as a woman much younger, blonde, tanned and dripping in gold and big nails.*)

VERA Hiya, I can't stop. I've gotta go check on the marquee, you know what hired help's like. You have to practically stand over 'em before they do the job properly. Anyway, I'll be back as quick as I can . . . where's Pam?

MANDY She's come to her senses and run away, Vera . . .

VERA Eh?

JOHNNY She's just nipped to Fletcher's.

MANDY She's fetching me a low-cal mixed salad on rye.

VERA Oh . . . right, good. I've just brought her pearls, she left 'em . . .

(*She's holding a jewelry case.* MANDY *smiles tightly.* VERA *looks at the shrine.*)

VERA What the hell's this?

MANDY It's a sort of gay shrine, Vera!

JOHNNY (*thrown*) It's a tribute to Diana!

MANDY (*sarcastic*) And the frame's solid silver from Saks New York!

VERA I don't care if it's solid gold and from Harrods – not today, eh?

JOHNNY But today is . . .

VERA I know what today is, thank you . . .

JOHNNY But Vera, it's purely out of love and respect . . .

VERA No, Johnny. Today it's out of order – so shift it!

(VERA *pulls him roughly aside and lowers her voice.*)

Today is my only son's wedding day . . . and the best day of mine and Pam's life.

(JOHNNY *looks her straight in the eyes – making her self-conscious.*)

JOHNNY Yes, I do know that, Vera.

VERA Good. Well, make sure you pamper Pammy. Let her have anything she wants . . .

MANDY What about me? Can I be pampered as well, Vera?

VERA Only if he's got time . . .

(VERA *exits.*)

JOHNNY I'm not moving it!

MANDY (*laughs*) You will . . .

JOHNNY I won't! She's lucky I'm even here . . . I didn't want to be.

MANDY Rubbish, you're milking Vera for all she's worth.

JOHNNY Do you think Pam's making a mistake?

MANDY Inviting her mother?

JOHNNY You know full well what I mean . . .

(MANDY *avoids him.*)

MANDY Ere, I think you should add a few more candles!

(MANDY *opens the case with the pearls in it and takes them out.*)

MANDY Do you reckon these are real?

JOHNNY Knowing Vera, they're probably just expensive fakes.

MANDY Makes no difference, she won't wear them.

JOHNNY Why?

MANDY I just know she just won't, that's all . . . well, not if Sandra turns up.

(JOHNNY *looks at Diana's photo.*)

JOHNNY They reckon pearls mean tears, anyway . . .

(MANDY *looks at the shrine.*)

MANDY So do you reckon it was really – an accident, or what?

JOHNNY If you don't mind, I'd rather not discuss it.

MANDY What, you telling me you an't got an opinion?

JOHNNY I just don't wish to discuss it right now, thank you.

MANDY Oh, come on, Johnny, you obviously thought a lot about the woman . . . you telling me you don't find it all a little bit dodgy?

JOHNNY I hardly think dodgy is . . .

MANDY What?

JOHNNY The right word.

MANDY Well, enlighten me then.

JOHNNY I don't want to upset Pam on her big day and neither should you.

MANDY Pam's not here . . .

JOHNNY (*snaps*) How do I know why she was killed? It was a freak accident, a cruel twist of fate . . .

MANDY Yeah, right . . .

JOHNNY . . . who knows why anyone is taken from us . . . we have no say in it, do we? We can't bring 'em back . . . and we can't stop 'em from going . . . all we can do is love 'em whilst they're still with us. Unfortunately, we all seem to forget that . . . look, I've got things I need to be getting on with . . .

(MANDY *holds her tummy – strokes her bump.*)

MANDY Why do you think everyone's so upset? 'Cos I mean they are, aren't they? I don't understand it, me. I mean I know she was a princess an' that. Do you reckon it's 'cos she was so beautiful still? Maybe it's just because she was a mother?

JOHNNY All I know is princesses aren't supposed to die.

(SANDRA *enters, unbeknown to* JOHNNY *and* MANDY. SANDRA *is done up like a woman who's just done India.*)

SANDRA I think you've been reading too many fairy stories, sunshine!

(MANDY *and* JOHNNY *both swing around.*)

MANDY Sandra! Blimey are they bells? (*She looks at the bells around her ankles.*)

SANDRA Look at you . . . I take it you are expecting? (*She feels* MANDY's *belly.*)

MANDY I'm 'avin' twins . . .

SANDRA Congratulations! (*She kisses her.*) So where's she hiding, then?

MANDY Vera?

(SANDRA *looks around.* JOHNNY *stands, gobsmacked.*)

SANDRA Not her . . . Pam.

MANDY She's just nipped to fetch me a bacon butty . . . blimey, Sandra, you look so . . .

SANDRA Serene, slim and healthy?

MANDY Well . . . yeah . . . sort of . . . what does serene mean?

SANDRA It means I've had a spiritual awakening . . .

MANDY Oh, I see . . . right . . . that's nice . . . in't it, Johnny?

JOHNNY Very . . .

SANDRA So . . . how is she?

MANDY You know what Vera's like, she's in her element . . .

SANDRA I'm not talking about Vera . . .

JOHNNY Oh, Pam's, you know, a tiny bit nervous.

SANDRA Oh yeah? And who are you then? One of Mickey's little friends?

(JOHNNY *and* MANDY *are thrown by this.*)

JOHNNY I . . .

MANDY He's . . .

JOHNNY This is my salon . . . I'm seeing to all Pam's beauty and hair preparation.

SANDRA And Vera's footing the bill, yeah?

JOHNNY That's right . . . here, let me take your things. Can I get you a drink?

(MANDY *looks at* SANDRA, *waiting to see if she asks for anything alcoholic.*)

SANDRA Yeah, I'll have a very large . . . black coffee. Make it strong.

(MANDY *smiles – relieved.* JOHNNY *exits to the kitchen.* SANDRA *is growing sick of waiting.*)

MANDY Shall we put the telly on?

SANDRA No.

(SANDRA *wanders about, restless.* MANDY *watches her closely.*)

SANDRA I thought you said she wouldn't be long?

MANDY I didn't think she would be, she's only nipped to Fletcher's . . .

SANDRA Aye, via Paragon station . . .

MANDY Eh?

SANDRA Maybe she's come to her senses?

MANDY What do you mean?

SANDRA What do you think I mean?

MANDY She's really happy, Sandra . . . honest.

SANDRA Yeah . . . ?

MANDY Yeah.

SANDRA And what about Mickey, is he really happy, too?

MANDY 'Course he is, he's marrying your Pammy.

SANDRA To please Vera?

MANDY Eh? No . . . well, yeah, but . . .

SANDRA But what?

MANDY But nothing . . . they love each other, you know they do. They always have . . . she's gonna be the making of him, Sandra . . .

SANDRA Yeah? And who said that? Vera?

MANDY Oh, bloody hell, you an't come to spoil it . . . 'ave yer?

(SANDRA *smiles – looks at the shrine.*)

SANDRA If I'd wanted to ruin her day . . . I wouldn't have traveled thousands of miles to be here, now would I?

MANDY Er . . . no, I don't suppose you would.

SANDRA So . . . she's been seeing a lot of him then, has she?

MANDY Yeah, course she has . . . they're inseparable.

SANDRA Sort of joined at the hip, you mean?

MANDY Well, no . . . I mean, he does do his own thing and that, but . . .

(JOHNNY *comes back with the coffee.*)

SANDRA But only when he thinks he can get away with it, eh?

MANDY Look, she's been keeping him on the straight and narrow . . . an't she, Johnny?

JOHNNY I don't think it's any of my . . .

(PAM *enters.*)

Pam!

PAM Mam!

(SANDRA *turns around and looks at her –* MANDY *grabs her bacon butty.*)

MANDY Oooh, gimmie, gimme . . . ta . . .

SANDRA Hiya, kid . . .

(PAM *looks at her, stunned.*)

PAM Are they bloody bells?

(SANDRA *shakes her ankle.*)

SANDRA Why, are bells banned from this wedding, then?

PAM When was the last time you washed your feet?

SANDRA You look thin.

PAM You look like you need a good wash!

MANDY (*with her mouth full*) Your Mam's had a spiritual what's it, Pam!

PAM Yeah? Well, Vera's gonna be here soon . . .

SANDRA (*sarcastic*) I can hardly wait . . . does she know I'm coming?

(*Pause –* JOHNNY *and* MANDY *look at one another, worried.*)

PAM No . . . but whatever she does or says . . . well, I'm still glad you could make it, Mam . . . I think.

SANDRA I wouldn't have missed it for the world . . . come 'ere . . .

(*She smiles – opens her arms and* PAM *slowly goes over to hug her.* JOHNNY *and* MANDY *smile, relieved.*)

SANDRA I think I smell a bit . . . .

PAM I've missed you, Mam . . . actually you stink.

SANDRA I've been travelling for days . . .

PAM I won't ask what in . . .

(SANDRA *holds her tighter.*)

SANDRA You feel so small . . . like a little girl still . . .

(PAM *suddenly feels suffocated – she struggles to break free.*)

PAM Well, I'm not . . . I'm a grown woman about to be married!

(SANDRA *steps back.*)

SANDRA Yeah . . . I suppose you are . . .

(SANDRA *moves over to the shrine.*)

You should 'ave seen the airport . . . full of bloody fools flocking to London for her funeral.

JOHNNY They just want to pay their last respects . . . they believed in her!

SANDRA Yeah, I know . . . (*She smiles.*) That's why they're fools.

(VERA *dashes in, talking ten-to-the-dozen.*)

VERA I do not believe Beverley bloody Minster! Do you know they've only said we can't have the normal bells . . . I ask yer . . .

(SANDRA *turns around.*)

SANDRA And what's Beverly Minster without bells, eh?

VERA What the hell is she doing here!?

SANDRA What do you think I'm doing here?

PAM I was going to tell you, Vera . . .

VERA Yeah? And when was that gonna be, eh?

PAM Well . . . now, I suppose . . .

MANDY She was, Vera, honest . . .

JOHNNY Mandy, stay out of it . . .

MANDY But I –

(PAM *gives her a mucky look.* MANDY *finishes her butty.*)

VERA Well, I hope to God she's brought summat decent to wear.

SANDRA Depends what you consider decent.

(SANDRA *walks over to the settee.* VERA *watches her feet – the bells jangle.*)

VERA Johnny? Isn't it about time Pammy was in that beauty room?

JOHNNY Well, I . . .

PAM We've got ages still.

VERA Not now she's turned up.

PAM The cars won't be here till half three.

VERA (*she whispers loudly*) 'Ave you seen the state of them feet?

SANDRA Actually we were just about to watch the funeral, Vera . . . here, come and sit next to me . . . be like the old days, eh?

(*She pats a space on the settee next to her –* VERA *looks at it and turns her back on her.*)

VERA That bloody telly's staying off!

(SANDRA *takes hold of the remote and switches it on.* VERA *swings around, angry.*)

VERA I suppose you think that's clever?

SANDRA No, Vera, switching it on without a remote would 'ave been clever!

VERA See! She's hardly been here five minutes and already she's causing trouble! What on earth possessed you to invite her, Pam?

PAM Vera, she's my mother!

(SANDRA *smiles* – JOHNNY *moves quickly.*)

JOHNNY Right, Pam! I'm ready for you in the beauty room . . . Mandy, wipe that bacon fat off your chin and come and have a nail soak.

PAM But . . .

VERA Go on, Pam . . .

JOHNNY Pam?

MANDY I'd rather stay in here . . .

JOHNNY Mandy, move it, now!

(*They leave.* VERA *feels awkward and avoids looking at* SANDRA. *She wanders about, looking at the telly. After awhile she speaks.*)

VERA Since when have you cared about the Royal family?

SANDRA I don't . . . I want you to watch it . . .

VERA I don't want to watch it . . .

SANDRA No? You were glued to the telly when she got married.

VERA Turn it off!

SANDRA Why? Can't you bear fairytales with the wrong endings?

Vera — I'm not gonna listen to you.

Sandra — This is what happens when you marry the wrong man, Vera . . .

Vera — No, Sandra, this is what happens when you don't stand by him and take off with some foreign play boy . . . turn it off!

(Vera *snatches the remote off her and switches it off.* Vera *walks over to the shrine, perhaps lighting a cigarette with one of the candles.*)

Sandra — Bit of a bad omen, don't you think?

Vera — What? You turning up?

Sandra — Half the world's in tears . . .

Vera — Aye, well half the world's nowt to do with me, and I told him to shift this bloody thing!

Sandra — You're good at that, aren't you?

Vera — What are you on about?

Sandra — Making people get rid of things you don't like.

Vera — Obviously not as good as I thought, else you wouldn't be sat there, lady!

Sandra — Pam invited me.

Vera — God knows why . . .

Sandra — Because I'm her mother.

Vera — Some mother you are!

Sandra — And I wanted to be here . . .

Vera — To spoil everything?

(*Pause.*)

SANDRA No.

VERA Well keep your clever mouth shut and that telly off, then.

SANDRA Unlike everyone one else, I no longer jump when you click your fingers, Vera.

VERA Look, I know why you're here and I'm telling you straight, all that nonsense was a long time ago. (*She looks at* SANDRA *for a reaction.*) Things have changed . . . my Mickey and your Pam really want this wedding.

SANDRA I know, she said so in her letter.

VERA Did she? . . . (*She smiles tightly.*) Well, there you are, then.

SANDRA That's why I'm here.

VERA Oh, well . . . good.

SANDRA So how long were they together? You know, going out, before they got engaged?

VERA Why? (SANDRA *doesn't answer – just waits for* VERA.) Ages . . . a year or so.

SANDRA He came back from Manchester, and what? Just started going out with her?

VERA Yeah . . . 'cause he missed her, that's why he came back.

SANDRA And does he miss Manchester?

VERA Well he's stayed here, hasn't he?

SANDRA Are you sure he doesn't keep popping back for the odd night out with the boys?

VERA What? See! I knew it!

SANDRA So does he?

VERA Look, what ever you're thinking. It's wrong.

SANDRA He went to Manchester in the first place because I finally showed you what he was!

VERA So this is why you're really here, is it? To ruin that lass's life all over again?

SANDRA She's my daughter, I've got every right to protect her.

VERA Protect her? The only thing she's ever needed protecting from is you!

(*A beat.*)

SANDRA So tell her then, tell her the real reason I had to leave.

VERA And let her hate you more? Is that what you want?

SANDRA (*snaps*) That wouldn't have been hard . . . without me trying to seduce the poor lad.

VERA And my son left because you scared the bloody life out of him!

SANDRA You asked me to! Anyway, all I bloody did was kiss the lad – one kiss, 'cos you needed to know!

VERA One kiss with you in a basque and stilettos, that's enough to scare any normal lad!

(*A beat.*)

SANDRA Yeah, but he wasn't normal, was he?

VERA Something's are just . . . best left. He broke his father's heart!

SANDRA He broke my Pam's heart!

VERA Aye, and the whole bloody lot of you broke mine. (*Pause.*) Four years he stayed away . . . four years and no word . . . do you have any idea what that does to a mother?

SANDRA How would I know? I'm not a real mother, am I? Not according to you.

VERA And the social services . . .

(*A beat.*)

SANDRA Yeah alright, thanks, Vera.

VERA I'd been telling you for years you 'ad a drink problem.

SANDRA Aye, well I haven't now.

VERA No wonder she was always happier living with me!

(SANDRA *suddenly snaps.*)

SANDRA I never left just 'cos I 'ad a drink problem, and you know it. I had to leave my daughter because of a favour I did for you!

VERA All I know is my son left me because you scared the bloody life out of him!

SANDRA He scared his bloody self.

VERA Look, lady, I don't know why you're 'avin a go at me. You should feel lucky I never told her about you and my Mickey . . . poor lad.

SANDRA Vera, listen to yourself, will yer? You sound as if it had nothing to do with you. You wanted me to do it – you needed to know!

VERA I never made you!

SANDRA I only did it for you! (*Pause.*) We were best friends . . . I could see you needed to know. I did it for you, Vera, you've got to know that. I did it because we were best friends.

VERA (*cries*) I was drunk, I didn't mean it! – You! You couldn't wait to jump on the poor lad! You confused him! You turned his mind. You bloody terrified him! If he had leanings in that direction, it was down to you! You pushed him over the edge! If he is . . . was . . . then it's because of you!

SANDRA You can't even say the word, can you?

(*Pause.*)

VERA They bloody love each other . . .

SANDRA I'm sure they do . . .

VERA What?

SANDRA She's known him since he was a kid . . .

VERA Exactly, and I think she knows him very well, don't you?

SANDRA So do they sleep together?

VERA What?

SANDRA You heard.

VERA (*snaps*) Marriage is about a hell of a lot more than sex, lady!

SANDRA What's wrong Vera, your George still not giving you any?

VERA (*jumps up*) I'm not gonna let you spoil this wedding!

SANDRA I'll take that as 'no' then, shall I?

VERA They've been saving themselves!

SANDRA (*laughs*) What the hell for? The big wedding night? When he breaks her heart 'cos she's got the wrong bits?

(VERA *slaps her face.* SANDRA *slaps her back. They grab each other's hair and struggle a bit.*)

VERA Gerr off me . . . ugh, you stink . . .

SANDRA You let go first . . .

VERA No . . . Ow . . . I said gerr off me . . . bloody India's made you worse!

SANDRA Not until you admit I'm right!

VERA Never! Do you ever wash?

(PAM *walks back on with the veil in the box.*)

PAM Mam, I . . . just wanted to show you my veil . . .

(VERA *and* SANDRA *let go of one another – trying to look innocent.*)

VERA (*smiles tightly*) I was just suggesting your mother took a shower.

SANDRA Well, come on then, let's see it . . .

PAM Is everything alright?

SANDRA Yeah . . . we were just remembering the good old days, wasn't we, Vera?

VERA Yeah. Well, come on then, don't leave your mother in suspense . . . let her see it . . . Pammy?

(PAM *starts to take it out but suddenly stops.*)

PAM No . . . look, I'll wait till me hair's done . . . and then you'll get a better picture.

(MANDY *shouts from off stage.*)

MANDY Pam! Get 'im off me, he's attacking me eyebrows!

PAM I better get back . . .

(*She quickly leaves.*)

VERA Now look what you've done, you've upset her!

SANDRA Vera, she's my only daugher . . . I've not come back to hurt her.

VERA No?

(*A beat.*)

SANDRA Of course not. I love her . . .

VERA Aye . . . 'course you do, well, we all do . . . she's a lovely girl . . .

SANDRA I know.

VERA And she looks like a proper princess in her dress, it's beautiful . . . she's gonna take our Mickey's breath away.

SANDRA And it was dead expensive, right?

VERA She's worth every penny, she's got a heart of gold, 'as that girl.

SANDRA Yeah, I know . . . that's what I'm afraid of.

(*Blackout. End of Act One.*)

ACT TWO

Scene One

In the darkness, Kraftwerk's The Model *plays. As the lights rise,* PAM, VERA, SANDRA *and* MANDY *are seated on tall stools facing opposite directions. They are wearing gowns and have their hair scooped up in towels. They have white opaque face packs on. They flick through the pages of* French Vogue – *in coordinated movement.*

The Queen's speech is inter-cut with the song. It comes in during the instrumental bits.

THE QUEEN "First I want to pay tribute to Diana myself. She was an exceptional and gifted human being. In good times and bad, she never lost her capacity to smile and laugh, nor to inspire others with warmth and kindness. I admired and respected her – for her energy and commitment to others, and especially for her devotion to her two boys."

(*Instrumental.*)

"No one who knew Diana will ever forget her. Millions of others who never met her, but felt they knew her, will remember her. I, for one, believe that there are lessons to be drawn from her life and from the extraordinary and moving reaction to her death – May those who died rest in peace and may we, each and every one of us, thank God for someone who made many people happy."

Scene Two

PAM, VERA, SANDRA *and* MANDY *are still in face packs. When they speak they try not to move their faces or mouths. An awkward silence.* JOHNNY *enters.*

JOHNNY Right – be careful not to crack those faces, girls.

MANDY How long we gotta sit like this? How the hell am I gonna snack?

JOHNNY You're not! These aren't your ten-a-penny packet masks, Mandy! These ingredients have come straight from the rain forest and are exclusively prepared for this salon.

MANDY They smell like Body Shop to me.

JOHNNY (*snaps*) Well trust me, they are most certainly not!

VERA (*snaps*) They had better not be!

JOHNNY Right, Sandra, perhaps you'd like to join me in the beauty room?

SANDRA What for?

VERA To get them feet in soak, for a start.

JOHNNY Mandy? If you could waddle this way, too.

(MANDY *follows him* – SANDRA *holds back.*)

MANDY Can I have a nap on the beauty bed?

JOHNNY Why? What do you think that's gonna achieve?

(*They exit* – SANDRA *looks at* VERA *then* PAM.)

SANDRA If you need me, Pam, you know where I am . . .

VERA She's managed for the past five years, what makes you think she's gonna need you now?

SANDRA Ask her the real reason she's invited me today.

PAM Go on, go and get sorted, Mam . . . please.

SANDRA — Are you sure?

PAM — I'm fine . . . really.

(SANDRA *exits.*)

VERA — And what the hell does she mean by that?

PAM — Vera, you're not meant to be talking with that on . . .

(VERA *picks at the face pack – which is now flaking.*)

VERA — Why didn't you tell me you wanted to invite her?

PAM — You didn't ask me. You just assumed I wouldn't be.

VERA — I didn't want to upset you . . . I didn't even know you had her address.

PAM — She wrote to me a few times.

VERA — (*thrown*) Oh well, that's nice . . . I'm glad. (*Pause.*) I just wish you'd told me, that's all. (*Pause.*) So, does our Mickey know she's coming?

PAM — Of course he does, we don't have any secrets from each other, Vera, not anymore.

VERA — That's 'cos you're completely suited to one another . . . me and my George, we're thrilled for you both, you do know that, don't you?

(*She squeezes* PAM'S *hand.*)

PAM — Yeah . . . 'course we do.

VERA — He's very special is our Mickey, isn't he?

PAM Yeah . . .

VERA A lot of people don't understand him like we do, do they?

PAM No.

VERA Your mother hardly knows him, really . . . I mean, the kind of man he is now, she just remembers how he was when he was, well, you know, young and foolish, that's all . . . 'ere, was your face itching a bit, you know, when he put this stuff on you?

PAM No.

VERA Johnny! (*Pause.*) I don't think she realises that a lot of young men struggle with their sexuality during puberty.

PAM (*half laughs to hide her embarrassment*) Vera!

VERA It's true, I've read about it. Not having a son, how can you expect her to understand – did you get a sort of tingling . . . ?

PAM No.

(VERA *scratches her face a bit.*)

VERA I've got hypo-sensitive skin, you know, so's our Mickey, well 'course you know that, don't you? (*She laughs nervously.*) I hope I don't come out in a bloody rash – what the hell did she mean, "the real reason" you invited her?

PAM I don't know, Vera.

(*She looks at* VERA'S *face – completely flaking now.*)

VERA She's allus been full of clever bloody words, 'as your mother – what you looking at? Oh, bloody hell, 'as it gone blotchy?

PAM No . . . well, it's a tiny bit red, but that's normal . . . I think . . .

VERA Eh? Oh 'eck, it's really itching, are you sure yours didn't?

PAM No . . . you better go and see Johnny, Vera.

(VERA *paces up and down, winding herself up and panicking about her face.*)

VERA I don't like to leave you in 'ere on your own, but I do think I need to get this off! Pam, promise me one thing . . .

PAM Look, I think you should go and get it sorted, Vera!

VERA Eh? . . . oh, bloody hell, Johnny! (*Panicking.*) Pam, don't look back, love . . . no matter what your mother says, that lad bloody adores you, he bloody worships you, Pammy, you know he does, don't you? (PAM *nods yes.*) Oh, where the hell is he? Johnny!

PAM Vera, I had to ask me Mam to come . . . you do understand, don't you?

VERA Frankly, Pam, no I don't – oh soddin' hell, if I've got one single blemish I swear to God I'll sue.

(VERA *dashes off to the beauty room.* PAM *walks over to the shrine and finds the box with the pearl necklace in it. She opens it and takes it out and tries it on briefly before replacing it in the box and hiding it behind the Diana frame. Left alone,* PAM *dozes on the reception settee.* SANDRA *enters and sits on the arm, watching her. The lighting denotes a short passing of time, and as* PAM *wakes, stretching – she opens her eyes to see her mother. She jumps up, panicking about the time.*)

PAM — Oh 'eck, I was miles away! What time is it?

SANDRA — You're alright, don't panic . . .

PAM — How long you been there?

SANDRA — Since you dropped off.

PAM — (*uncomfortable*) Staring at me?

SANDRA — (*strokes hair out of* PAM'S *eyes*) No . . . just taking you in . . .

(SANDRA *moves away – she can see* PAM *feels pressured by her affection.*)

PAM — Is Vera still in the beauty room?

SANDRA — Yeah . . . let's face it, she needs all the time she can get in there.

(*They both laugh – awkward. A pause.*)

PAM — I can't believe you're here.

SANDRA — No? . . . I can hardly believe it meself.

PAM — I do understand why you went, you know . . . I just don't know why you stayed away so long.

SANDRA — Maybe there's nothing to understand . . . that's the way it worked out, that's all . . .

PAM — Actually, that's not the truth . . . I've never really understood why you left . . . I mean Vera said it's 'cos you wanted to get off the booze and the doctor recommended it . . . (*She looks at* SANDRA.) She said it was either India or the funny farm.

SANDRA — That's one way of putting it . . .

PAM — I just don't understand why you left so quickly, especially when you knew how upset we both were when Mickey left home.

SANDRA — I left because I really had no choice. They'd already taken you off me once. Vera was my way out.

PAM — Out of my life?

(*Pause.*)

SANDRA — To give you the life you deserved.

PAM — Vera said that you told her she'd allus been a far better mother to me than you ever was . . .

SANDRA — I did . . .

PAM — She said it wasn't actually a selfish act on your part, it was the opposite . . . that you sacrificed your happiness for me to have a better life with her and George.

SANDRA — Why? Don't you think that's true?

PAM — Not really . . . how can you sacrifice something you don't actually have?

SANDRA — What do you mean?

PAM — You didn't sacrifice your happiness, did you? You were never happy.

SANDRA — I was unhappy with myself, Pam. Not you.

PAM — I know . . . that's why Mickey said he left.

SANDRA — And is he happy with himself now?

PAM — Are you?

SANDRA — I've stopped drinking myself senseless, but then I had to face the fact that I've probably hurt you as much as myself . . .

PAM — I know. So you said in your letters . . . amazing, isn't it? You screw our lives up for fifteen years, disappear for five and send me three letters telling me something I already knew. You was a crap mother.

(*Pause.*)

SANDRA — Well, Vera's more than made up for it, hasn't she?

PAM — Yeah . . . in a sort of Vera way. (*Pause.*) When Mickey left home she was devastated, you know . . . but when you left she seemed to get stronger. I think it was for my sake.

SANDRA — She paid for me to leave, Pam.

PAM — Yeah? Well, I guessed as much.

SANDRA — And when Mickey came back, how was Vera then?

PAM — How do you think? She was over the moon, we both were.

SANDRA — I bet you were.

PAM — I still am.

SANDRA — Has he told you why he left?

PAM — Yes, of course he has, I told you in my letter.

SANDRA — Tell me again.

PAM — He wanted to live a bit . . . find out what he wanted from life . . .

SANDRA — And did he?

PAM — Sort of . . . but I always knew that just like when we were kids he'd come back and marry me . . . no matter what, he never stopped loving me . . .

SANDRA — Why do you think I left around the same time as Mickey?

PAM — (*snaps*) I don't know, and does all this matter now?

SANDRA — You tell me.

PAM — Look, all I know is Mickey's not gonna run off and leave me again!

SANDRA — How?

PAM — Because in a few hours' time I'm gonna be his wife! Alright?

SANDRA — Why did you really ask me to come, Pam?

PAM — (*half laughs*) Why do you think?

SANDRA — I want you to tell me.

PAM — Maybe I can't.

(JOHNNY *walks back in from the beauty room.* PAM *is aware of him.*)

PAM — Because you're me Mam, and I want you to see me in me wedding dress . . .

SANDRA — Is that the only reason . . . Pam?

(PAM *stands and walks towards* JOHNNY.)

PAM — Why? Isn't that good enough? (*To* JOHNNY.) How they doing, Johnny – is Mandy behaving?

(JOHNNY *is holding the veil box.*)

JOHNNY Well, I have just had to save this from 'er grubby mits . . . she's stuffed her face so much she's got belly ache now. She was only after trying this on!

PAM That must have pleased Vera.

(*Pause.*)

JOHNNY Vera's . . . quiet, actually.

(SANDRA *leaves.*)

SANDRA I bet she is . . . she's not the only one.

(*Blackout.*)

Scene Three

The lights rise on JOHNNY *taking the curlers out of Pam's hair – they have the telly on in front of them – with the sound turned down.* PAM *is close to tears.*

JOHNNY Is it upsetting you? I can turn it off if you like.

PAM No, you're alright. (*Pause.*) All those people though, Johnny . . . I mean, how often do you see that many people . . . all pulling together? I mean, I know it's out of summat bad, but I dunno . . . it does summat to you, doesn't it?

JOHNNY Yeah, it does.

PAM I wonder if she knows? Wherever she is . . . I wonder if she knows what's she's done to the world . . . how sad we all are?

JOHNNY When my Jimmy was dying . . . none of his family came to see him, except his mother and even then she was telling everyone he had cancer. She was scared what people thought, you see . . .

PAM 'Cos he had Aids?

JOHNNY Yeah . . . and 'cos they hadn't told anyone about us.

PAM Oh. (*Pause.*) That's awful.

JOHNNY Then Diana was all over the papers, do you remember, it was 1991. . . holding the hands of that man with Aids . . .

PAM Yeah . . . yeah, I think I do.

JOHNNY His mother turned up the next day and told us she was ashamed of herself, said she was going to tell everyone the truth . . .

PAM That he had Aids?

JOHNNY Yeah, and that he was gay.

PAM That was brave of her.

JOHNNY We never saw her again . . . I think her husband must have stopped her.

PAM Families . . . they don't half fuck us up, don't they?

JOHNNY Only if you let them . . .

PAM Do you think it's a shame that gay men can't get married . . . I mean legally an' that?

JOHNNY We never felt the need to . . . we were happy and together and that's all that mattered.

PAM I suppose if there was no such thing as marriage people would still live together and have kids an' that. I mean a lot people don't even bother, do they?

JOHNNY No . . . they don't.

PAM Me Mam was asking me about when Mickey was in Manchester, you know, even Vera was going on about his 'leanings' when he was younger . . . I don't know why they're making such a big deal about it, do you?

JOHNNY That's mothers for you . . .

PAM I mean, I know he hung around with poofs, he's never denied that, has he?

JOHNNY No.

PAM Vera knows he keeps in touch with them, I've even met some of them and they're nice blokes. Some are a bit over the top for me, but that doesn't mean anything, does it?

JOHNNY No.

PAM I mean loads of people have gay friends, Marion at our place lives with a woman who looks like a docker, so what? She still comes out with us all.

JOHNNY Maybe your mam just worries that . . . (*He stops himself.*) I don't think she believes you love him, deep down.

PAM What?

JOHNNY Oh I don't know, maybe you should just ask her straight.

PAM She doesn't know anything, how can she? She's been in bloody India.

JOHNNY She thinks Mickey's gay, Pam.

(PAM *laughs.*)

PAM I know! She might be off the booze but she's still mad! I think I would know if my future husband was a poof, don't you?

(*She looks at* JOHNNY – *his face gives him away.*)

PAM Oh, don't look like that Johnny, what is it about you lot, eh? Vera's bloody right, you think all good-looking men are queer!

JOHNNY Oh, please . . .

PAM It's true!

JOHNNY Let's just change the subject, shall we . . .

PAM Why?

JOHNNY Because . . . I'm really not the best person to discuss Mickey's sexuality, alright?

PAM What you saying it like that for?

JOHNNY Like what?

PAM Like you think he is!

JOHNNY Pam, you know what you have between you . . . if you both want to get married then that's what you should do. Marry him and be happy . . . OK?

PAM Yeah. (*Pause.*) We've never done it, you know.

JOHNNY Well, I'm sure you'll do it tonight.

PAM I bloody hope so . . . he is sexy, isn't he?

JOHNNY Yes, he is, and you're beautiful . . .

PAM When did you know your Jimmy really loved you, Johnny?

JOHNNY When he walked away from his family, to be with me. (*Pause.*) Even though he knew he could never go back.

PAM Did he miss them?

JOHNNY Yes, 'course he did, but not enough to live a lie.

PAM Do you think Mickey came back because he missed us? Me?

JOHNNY I know he did.

PAM And if we get married?

JOHNNY If?

Pam Do you think he'd be living a lie?

(*Pause.*)

JOHNNY I think he would be, Pam . . . and deep down I think Vera knows it, too.

(MANDY *comes on groaning and holding her belly.*)

MANDY Oh don't worry about me, whatever you do . . .

JOHNNY Don't worry, we're not.

PAM Why don't you go and take the weight of your feet for bit. We've got ages still.

JOHNNY Yeah, you don't want them ankles any bigger now, do you?

MANDY What's going on?

PAM Nothing.

MANDY Vera and your mother are killing each other with mucky looks in there and now you've got a face like a wet week . . . you been watching her funeral or summat? (*She doubles up.*) Oh eck, maybe you're right . . . If you want me I'll be kipping on the beauty bed.

JOHNNY Aye, well, make sure you don't touch 'owt. I'll be through in a bit to check!

(*A beat.*)

PAM I invited me Mam so she'd come and put an end to it all. (*Pause*). Stop the wedding.

(*Pause.*)

JOHNNY I know you did, and so does Vera . . . but . . .

PAM But what?

JOHNNY Wouldn't it be quicker and less time consuming if you did it yourself . . . like now, 'cos I swear to God, Pam, I don't think I can take much more of this . . . not today.

(PAM *ignores him – she's in a world of her own.*)

PAM Why hasn't she done something, Johnny?

JOHNNY 'Cos she knows that this late in the day, well, it's a massive thing to do, isn't it? She probably needs you to ask her. She has to know it's what you want. (*Pause.*) She's just waiting for you, Pam. If it's really what you want you have to say something and soon.

PAM (*tough*) Yeah? Well she can bloody wait . . . they both can. This is my day and I'll spoil it when I'm good and ready.

(*She smiles.* JOHNNY *looks at her.*)

JOHNNY Pam, I really think that attitude isn't going to help matters . . . it's not like you, and if you don't mind me saying so it's a little bit scary. I . . .

(VERA *dashes on, checking the colour of her newly painted nails, followed by* SANDRA.)

JOHNNY Oh 'eck . . . (*He smiles tightly.*) Vera, what can I do for you?

VERA 'Ere, are you sure this colour won't clash with me wedding outfit?

SANDRA Why what colour is it?

VERA (*snaps*) Like you give a knack?

(PAM *tuts.*)

JOHNNY (*in a flap*) Vera, you know I'm a colour co-ordination perfectionist – now, get those nails dried before they flippin' well smudge, lady, and Sandra, it's time you got those feet in soak!

(*He guides* VERA *to the nail drier.*)

VERA (*under her breath*) Aye, they'll need at least an hour. (*Gushing.*) Oh Pammy, your hair looks gorgeous, doesn't it look gorgeous, Sandra?

SANDRA (*flat*) Yeah, it does.

PAM (*flat*) Thanks.

(JOHNNY *senses the atmosphere and tries to be light – as he switches on the foot spa.*)

JOHNNY Right, plonk your feet in there. I've blended together three rare oils of the Orient for inner calm. So try not to splash. Everyone happy?

(*He looks at both* SANDRA *and* VERA *– clearly not happy about been left alone together.*)

JOHNNY Marvellous. Right, Pam, now let's get that face sparkling, shall we?

(SANDRA *shouts after* PAM *as she exits.*)

SANDRA I know you're avoiding me!

VERA I don't blame her!

JOHNNY Actually, she's avoiding you both.

(*He exits.*)

SANDRA She's not daft, she knows we're rowing.

VERA No one's rowing. It takes two to row and I've got nothing to say to you.

(*Uncomfortable with herself, she switches the nail dryer off and paces the floor, smoking –* SANDRA *watches her.*)

VERA My Mickey's always been a gentle boy. Kind. Loving. Good to his mother . . . he always says me hair looks nice . . . even when me roots needed doing.

SANDRA Oh don't lie to yourself, Vera.

VERA Ah, shurr-up . . . living these days is all lies. Look at that poor girl . . . (*She looks at the photo of Diana.*) She was a bloody Princess. She had everything. Everything . . . and even she was living a big fat lousy lie!

(SANDRA *waits for* VERA *to react.*)

VERA I hope you know the *Journal* are sending their best society photographer . . .

(SANDRA *ignores her.*)

VERA Not just anybody can get Beverley Minster, you know . . .

SANDRA Oh, fuck Beverley Minster!

VERA You think it's that easy, do you?

(SANDRA *turns the foot spa off.*)

SANDRA I know you want your big day. (*Sarcastic.*) I'm sure your new society friends are *very* impressed with it all, Vera. But a bit of bloody glory for one day isn't worth a lifetime of misery. Our Pam doesn't deserve that, you know she doesn't!

VERA What would you know about misery? Swannin' about the world with bloody bells on your ankles? I'll tell you what misery is. Painting on a smile everyday and pretending it's real . . . looking at yourself in the mirror and pretending it's beautiful and real . . .

SANDRA You used to smile and mean it.

VERA Yeah? Now I just cough and pee meself. Joke.

(*She stands and moves towards the shrine.*)

I had me hair done like hers for ages, you know. It quite suited me. Everyone said so. I was once walking into Hammonds and this old woman stopped me and squeezed my hand. She never said anything but I knew she thought I was Diana. I could see it in her eyes. It made me feel so . . . loved, suddenly. Just for a few seconds. I think she was a bit confused or something, I mean I hardly look like her, do I?

SANDRA No, you don't.

VERA (*put out*) And, anyway, she did smell of urine.

SANDRA She'll be out here soon and I'm telling you straight – that veil is not coming out that box!

VERA That's right, break her bloody heart all over again!

SANDRA She's probably only going through with it to please you!

VERA And what do I say to everyone, eh? That I had to cancel because my son's . . .

SANDRA Gay.

(VERA *sits, deflated.*)

SANDRA It's hard for you to admit. I know it is. But today's all wrong and you know it!

VERA Look at you! No make-up, no stockings . . . You think you've got something, don't you? I can see it in your eyes. You think you've suddenly got all the right answers, don't you?

SANDRA I've had a great big spoonful of soul searching. That's all.

VERA (*laughs*) What the fuck does that mean?

SANDRA It means I've taken a good look at the woman I am within.

VERA Within? What about without? Your hair's buggered. Your ends are shocking . . .

SANDRA None of that matters.

VERA (*laughs*) None of that matters? (*Snaps.*) To you, maybe. You gadding about soddin' India! But you wanna try living in the real world for a bit. Do you think it's easy to hit fifty and still look forty? Eh? Do you?

(*A beat.*)

Well it's not. It's bloody hard work and it's expensive.

(SANDRA *looks at her and sighs.*)

VERA Everyday a new product is dangled in front of me face promising me eternal youth. I buy it and I spread it on. And then I wait and wait and bloody wait for this miracle of science to take place but there's no such things as bloody miracles! Not in Hull, anyway.

SANDRA Oh, so we're talking about you again, are we? Only I did think this was actually about two young people about to ruin their lives!

(*A beat.*)

VERA We've come to the end of the road. Me and my George – it's over. He's not the man he was.

SANDRA What?

VERA The wedding's his guilt money. It's our last big show of wealth, success and a marvellous bloody marriage.

(PAM *walks on. She's still in a gown. Her make-up has been applied and her face looks beautiful.*)

PAM Mam . . . ?

SANDRA (*moved*) Oh, Pam . . .

(*They hug. Pull back.* VERA *looks nervous.*)

VERA Your face looks nice . . . very pretty.

PAM Ta . . .

(JOHNNY *walks on carrying the veil in the box.*)

JOHNNY Well, ladies, is this coming out yet? Pam? (*He looks at* PAM.)

PAM Er, no . . . no not without Mandy here.

JOHNNY Well, Mandy's still out of it on the beauty bed.

VERA 'Ere, Pam, I was just telling your mother about my poor George. About his attack . . .

SANDRA (*snaps*) Attack? You never mentioned anything about an attack!

VERA (*snaps*) No, well I am now!

JOHNNY Oooh 'eck, Vera, was it his heart?

VERA No Johnny, it was from behind.

JOHNNY Oh dear . . .

VERA Mugged outside his Lodge last February. Valentine's Day, actually. Left for dead face down in a kebab.

JOHNNY Oh, nasty . . .

VERA He hasn't been the same man since . . .

JOHNNY I bet he hasn't . . .

(*A beat.*)

PAM Why are you lying, Vera? You don't have to lie to me Mam.

(*They all look at* VERA.)

VERA It was a bad attack!

JOHNNY From behind?

PAM No. It was a heart attack.

JOHNNY Oh . . . and the kebab?

PAM It was another woman.

JOHNNY Oh?

PAM He was in another woman's bed.

JOHNNY Eating a kebab?

PAM Not exactly . . .

JOHNNY Oh? . . . oooh!

VERA Though I do understand that in her case the smell is very similar . . .

(JOHNNY *and* PAM *try not to laugh.* SANDRA *is less amused.*)

VERA No, she did me a favour! It brought my Mickey home and that's all that matters now – isn't that right, Pam?

(*There is an uncomfortable silence.*)

PAM Yeah . . . (*Pause.*)

(PAM *and* JOHNNY *speak at the same time.*)

PAM Vera . . .

JOHNNY Oh, Pam, I almost forgot! I've got a lovely bottle of bubbly ready to crack open when the veil goes on. Do you mind helping me with the glasses, Pam?

PAM Er . . . yeah. Yeah.

(*They exit.*)

SANDRA So who is she – this other woman?

VERA She's younger than me. Beautiful in his eyes. Men love beautiful, it makes them weak. They love looking into beautiful eyes and seeing a reflection of themselves younger, brighter –

better. They don't see strong. They don't see love like an anchor. Grounding us in loyalty. They don't see what we see . . . the way we love them . . . even if he is an old fool. They just see a woman whose face isn't beautiful anymore. (*Pause.*) I just wanted him to stop. Stop and tell me it doesn't matter. Bloody hell, he'd save himself a fortune.

(*She retouches her lipstick, powders her nose* – SANDRA *watches her. She sprays herself with perfume, moves over to* SANDRA *and sprays it in her direction* – SANDRA *looks at her and smiles warmly.*)

VERA I'm not like you! I haven't done India. If I stopped wearing all this, they'd think we were hard up. You make me cancel this wedding and my life is over!

SANDRA You're wrong, Vera. Do the right thing and I promise you, you'll feel like a new woman. Give them kids a chance to be happy.

VERA Happy? You make it sound easy.

SANDRA I know it's not easy. (*Pause.*) But I'm here. I'll back you up.

VERA Haven't you gotta get back to bloody India?

SANDRA I've done India. Now it's time I did Hull. The right way.

(VERA *looks at Diana's picture. Lifts it up and holds it to her heart. She puts it back. Turns back.*)

VERA I lied.

SANDRA Eh? Again? (*Laughs.*) How many lies can one woman tell in a day?

(*They both smile.*)

VERA She's not beautiful. Or young. She's not even blonde.

SANDRA Who?

VERA The other woman. The one he loves. Loves?! Can you believe that? Thirty years of bloody marriage and he never says he loves anything. Not even me. Not even Mickey. I ask him, I say, do you like my hair, George? He says, yes . . . he likes it. What about my outfit, George? Yes, Vera, it's very nice . . . well what about me, George, eh? You red-faced, bald headed, short-arsed little runt – eh? What about me! I might be able to understand it if she was at least a little bit attractive. But she's fat, Sandra. Fat, fifty, frumpy and posh. Proper posh. Born fucking posh – you know? (*Pause.*) I'm just not . . .

SANDRA No, you're not.

VERA Yeah? Well aren't I the bloody lucky one, eh?

(JOHNNY *and* PAM *enter with the champagne.*)

PAM Before we pop the cork . . . well . . . I . . . I think we'd better wake sleeping beauty, don't you? She'd hate to miss this . . .

(*They suddenly hear a blood-curdling scream coming from the beauty room. They all look at one another –* MANDY *suddenly shouts.*)

MANDY Pam! I think I've peed on the beauty bed . . . either that or me waters have broke! Oh 'eck!

(*Blackout.*)

Scene Four

JOHNNY *is on his own – lit by just the glow of the candles – he's praying.* SANDRA *enters.*

SANDRA Say one for me an' all, will you?

(VERA *enters.*)

SANDRA Better make it two . . .

VERA Where's that champagne? I've never seen a bloody birth so quick – they couldn't wait to get out, could they?

JOHNNY And I wonder why . . . Right! I'll get that cork popped!

VERA Don't think you're getting any, 'cos you're not!

SANDRA Oh shurr-up, Vera.

VERA Ah, shurr-up yourself. I wish Pam'd hurry up and get back, our Mickey's gonna be here soon . . .

SANDRA (*smiles*) I thought it was unlucky for the groom to see the bride before the wedding?

VERA Na, that's the bleedin' mother-in-law.

SANDRA So was that a tear I saw in the hospital?

VERA Childbirth is a very moving experience.

SANDRA I'm sure Mandy might agree with you one day.

VERA Poor lass, it's bad enough bringing one into the bloody world, never mind two!

SANDRA Do the right thing, Vera, when Mickey gets here, put an end to all this, eh?

(VERA *is looking for the box of pearls.*)

VERA — I'll put and end to you in a minute. Who's moved that box with the pearls in? . . . He's taking his time with that champagne . . . where the hell is that box?

SANDRA — Calm down.

VERA — Calm down? They're not fakes you know, they're bloody antiques, they're her something old . . . I know I left the box on 'ere . . . (*She finds it behind the framed photo of Diana.*) She's still got a little battered heart, you know . . . your Pam.

SANDRA — (*snaps*) And I suppose you think that's my fault?

VERA — Well, you gave her it! (*Pause – softer.*) It's got a picture of you in it . . . sober . . . it must be a bloody old one . . .

(JOHNNY *comes back with the champagne – hands a glass to* VERA, *gives* SANDRA *orange.*)

JOHNNY — Well, ladies, here's to new life, eh?

VERA — Aye, I suppose so . . . new life!

SANDRA — (*looks at* VERA) And new beginnings . . .

VERA — Who shoved these pearls behind that frame, Johnny?

JOHNNY — I don't know, it wasn't me.

(PAM *walks on.*)

PAM — It was me, Vera.

JOHNNY — Pam! How's she doing?

SANDRA — If you need me, Pam . . . well, you know where I am, love.

PAM Yeah, I know.

(PAM *watches her exit.* VERA *sits down – deflated – holding the pearls.*)

VERA It felt like making love . . . but even gentle I knew it wasn't. His heart wasn't in it . . . (*She looks at the telly.*) I'd ring and cancel the flowers only I know it's too late. I'd ring and cancel the reception but that's too late an-all . . . Oh 'eck, what 'ave I done? (*She panics.*) What 'ave I gone and done?

(PAM *holds her.*)

I'm ashamed of meself, Pam – I've pushed you into all this, haven't I?

PAM Well . . . yes. (*She looks at her and cannot bring herself to be mean.*) No, not totally. I think we both just got a bit carried away, Vera . . . you know? For all the wrong reasons.

VERA I just wanted a happy ending . . . you looked so perfect in that wedding dress in the shop . . . like a real princess . . . everything I've always dreamed of.

PAM I know.

VERA I know you love Mickey, because he does love you, doesn't he?

PAM Yeah, he does . . . but not the way I need him to.

VERA They never do.(*She downs her drink in one and pours herself another.*) Oh, sod it, what do I care? It's his money we're gonna be chucking down the drain. Money he won't 'ave left to spend on Miss Snooty Drawers. (*Pause.*) No, I'll cancel the flowers, I'm sure they'll find a good use for 'em and George can sort the rest. So he loses a few thousand. He might even enjoy it – proving me wrong one last time.

(*A beat.*)

PAM What do you mean?

VERA He never wanted this wedding. Oh, it's nowt to do with the money. The big lump still believes in true love . . . summat we never had.

(*She looks at the picture of Diana and picks it up.*)

PAM Something a lot of people don't have.

VERA (*panics*) Oh, Pam, are you sure you can't go through with it? Just for the do, and that . . . then you can go on the honeymoon, get a nice tan and when you come back we can sort you a quickie divorce? No one needs to know.

PAM No, Vera, I can't . . . (*Pause.*) I don't think like that. I know Mandy's Dave in't the most bright bloke going . . . well, Mandy's not perfect either, but I saw the way he looked at her and the way he held them babies. Well, that's gotta be what life is about, in't it? That's when marriage takes on a whole new meaning, in't it? That's gotta be what loving someone is really about.

VERA Yeah, I suppose so. (*Pause.*) For the lucky ones . . .

(*A beat. Pam puts the picture back.*)

PAM Maybe for some people there's no such things as happy endings.

VERA (*tries to be light*) 'Course there is, well, for you there will be. I know it.

PAM You do know that Mickey will probably leave Hull now, don't you?

VERA Yeah. I feel like clearing off meself . . .

PAM Oh, Vera . . . I'm so sorry I've left it all so late. I should 'ave said summat sooner. It wan't that I was scared or owt . . . not really, I just couldn't ever find the right time and I know Mickey deserves the truth and so do you.

VERA We rarely get the things we think we deserve . . . to be honest, I thought Beverley Minster was a bit too good to be true . . .

PAM Cheer up, Vera. (*She smiles.*) Mandy said you can be godmother to her baby girl.

VERA Oh, aye, and who's gonna be godmother to the boy? Oh 'eck, not your bloody mother?

PAM No . . . (*She smiles.*) I am.

VERA Good . . . (*She giggles.*) Oh 'eck . . . all George's funny hand-shake-wives, Pam, all turning up in their best clobber expecting the do of the century!

PAM Yeah, but all been sent home with the best bit of gossip this town 'as ever heard!

VERA Aye. (*Grins.*) I think I'll blame George, tell 'em all he was in denial. Ah well, it's not all bad, is it, kid? (*Sarcastic.*) At least we've got your bloody mother back.

(*She laughs briefly, holds her glass up.*)

VERA 'Ere's to the delights of motherhood, let's hope at least one of 'em takes after their father, eh?

(PAM *smiles – she fills up.*)

VERA — Oh don't, Pammy . . . you'll set me off an-all. (*Pause.*) 'Ere, come here.

(*She holds her – They both look at the picture of Diana as* SANDRA and JOHNNY *return.*)

PAM — (*brave*) It's alright, Johnny . . . Mam . . . Vera's gonna get George to cancel the wedding.

(SANDRA *looks at* VERA *and smiles.*)

SANDRA — Right . . . good. So we can celebrate properly now!

VERA — Aye, well, there's still no champagne for you, lady.

(VERA *pours herself another glass – tops* JOHNNY'S *and* PAM'S *glasses up.*)

JOHNNY — (*beams*) Oh ta! I can't believe I'm gonna be godfather!

VERA — Eh? You?!

JOHNNY — Yes, Vera. Me!

PAM — Well he has promised Mandy free beauty treatment until he's sixteen!

VERA — He?! You're gonna be godfather to her son?

JOHNNY — Yes, that's right. Why, have you got a problem with that?

VERA — No . . . no course I haven't . . .

(*She picks up the photo of Diana and looks at it – places it back.*)

VERA — What a bloody day, eh?

SANDRA You rung George yet?

VERA No.

SANDRA Well, don't you think you should? The cars'll be here soon.

(VERA *holds her glass up and grins.* SANDRA *looks at her and they both laugh.* JOHNNY *fills their glasses.*)

PAM To Mandy and Baby Johnny!

VERA Eh? Why Johnny?

(JOHNNY *grins.*)

JOHNNY She's calling him after me, Vera!

VERA What the hell for?

JOHNNY Well, I did practically deliver 'em!

VERA Excuse me, sunshine, I held her bloody hand and I tell you that lass 'as got a grip like a bloody vice! So what's the girl gonna be called?

SANDRA Not Vera, that's for sure . . .

PAM . . . she's calling her Diana.

(*They all look at the shrine – raise their glasses.*)

ALL To Mandy, Johnny and Diana!

VERA Aye – God help em all!

(*Music kicks in. The lights fade as the music swells. Blackout.*)